W9-AFT-267

Oceans

Precious McKenzie

ROURKE PUBLISHING
www.rourkepublishing.com

www.rourkepublishing.com

PHOTO CREDITS: Cover: © Rich Carey; Title Page: © Iakov Kalinin; Page 5: © Jan Martin Will; Page 6: © NASA, © Wikipedia; Page 8: © Musimon, © gmnicholas; Page 9: René Mansi; Page 10: © AccesscodeHFM; Page 12: © snaprender, © NOAA; Page 13: © The United States Geological Survey, © nps; Page 14: © Kevin Panizza, © Petershort; Page 15: © RainervonBrandis; Page 16: © grandriver, © Paul Whitted; Page 17: © JodiJacobson; Page 18: © George Peters; Page 19: © GoldenLobby; Page 20: ©MsLightBox; Page 21: © leofrancini; Page 22: © bonniej, © Maica; Page Border: © Michaeljung

Edited by Kelli L. Hicks

Cover Design by Nicola Stratford   bdpublishing.com,
Interior Design by Renee Brady

Library of Congress Cataloging-in-Publication Data

McKenzie, Precious, 1975-
 Oceans / Precious McKenzie.
    p. cm. -- (Eye to eye with endangered habitats)
 Includes bibliographical references and index.
 ISBN 978-1-61590-314-6 (Hard Cover) (alk. paper)
 ISBN 978-1-61590-553-9 (Soft Cover)
 1. Oceans--Juvenile literature. I. Title.
 GC21.5.M3919 2011
 551.46--dc22
                                   2010009272

Rourke Publishing
Printed in the United States of America, North Mankato, Minnesota
033010
033010LP

www.rourkepublishing.com - rourke@rourkepublishing.com
Post Office Box 643328 Vero Beach, Florida 32964

Table of Contents

A Watery World 4

The Water We Share 6

Always on the Move 8

Currents. 10

Under the Water 12

Animals and Fish 14

Fun for Us! 16

Fishing and Farming 18

Drill! 20

Protecting Our Oceans 22

Glossary 23

Index. 24

A Watery World

Water covers ninety-seven percent of the Earth's surface. The largest bodies of water on our planet are called oceans. According to the International Hydrographic Organization, Earth has five oceans: the Pacific Ocean, the Atlantic Ocean, the Indian Ocean, the Arctic Ocean, and the Southern Ocean.

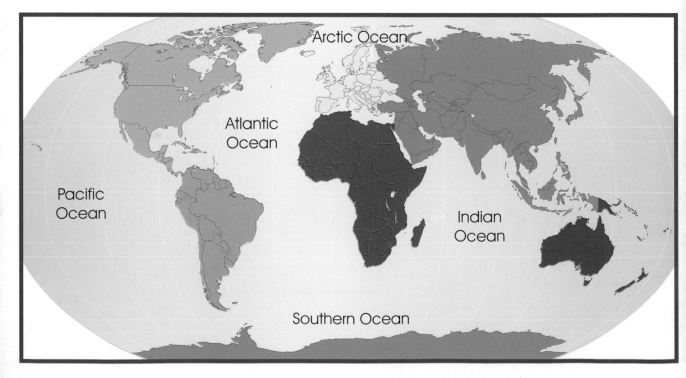

In 2000, scientists decided to name the water around Antarctica the Southern Ocean.

The Water We Share

Although we label the world's oceans by their **geographic** areas, scientists determined that all of the world's oceans are actually interconnected. All five oceans form one very large body of water. Even Earth's rivers, streams, lakes, and seas link to one global ocean.

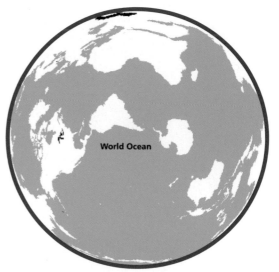

Russian oceanographer Yuly Shokalsky coined the phrase world ocean to describe the continuous body of water that covers most of the Earth.

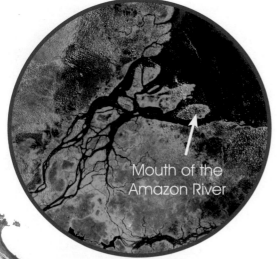

Mouth of the Amazon River

Sometimes scientists study water flow from satellite images. This image is of the mouth of the Amazon River.

All of the water on Earth participates in the same cycle.
Rain or snow from the sky falls to Earth, landing into the
ground and waterways. Eventually, water evaporates and
forms precipitation and the water cycle begins again.

Always on the Move

The pull of **gravity** from the Moon affects ocean tides. Tides change based on the rotation of the Earth and how close the Earth is to the Moon. At high tide, the water level rises. At low tide, the water level decreases. Earth has two cycles of high tide and low tide every twenty-four hours.

Without the Moon's pull of gravity, Earth would not have a regular tide schedule.

At low tide, children can explore tidal pools where they find small marine animals such as sea urchins and crabs.

One way to tell whether it is high tide or low → tide is to see how far the water comes ashore.

At high tide, the ocean water will rush farther up the beach.

At low tide, the ocean water will recede and there will be much more dry sand on the beach.

Currents

Currents move ocean water. When wind blows across the surface of the ocean, it forces the ocean water to move in large streams.

The Gulf Stream current begins in the Gulf of Mexico. It travels off the shore of Cape Hatteras and up the eastern coast of the United States. At its most northern route it travels past Newfoundland and Norway.

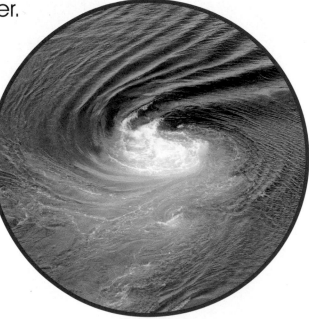

This aerial photo is of the Saltstraumen, the world's fastest current, near Norway. The inner circle of the current is about 30 feet (9.1 meters) in diameter.

*Many people pay close attention to ocean currents. Sailors and scientists track ocean currents to help them travel more efficiently. **Meteorologists** study ocean currents to determine the temperatures of coastal areas.*

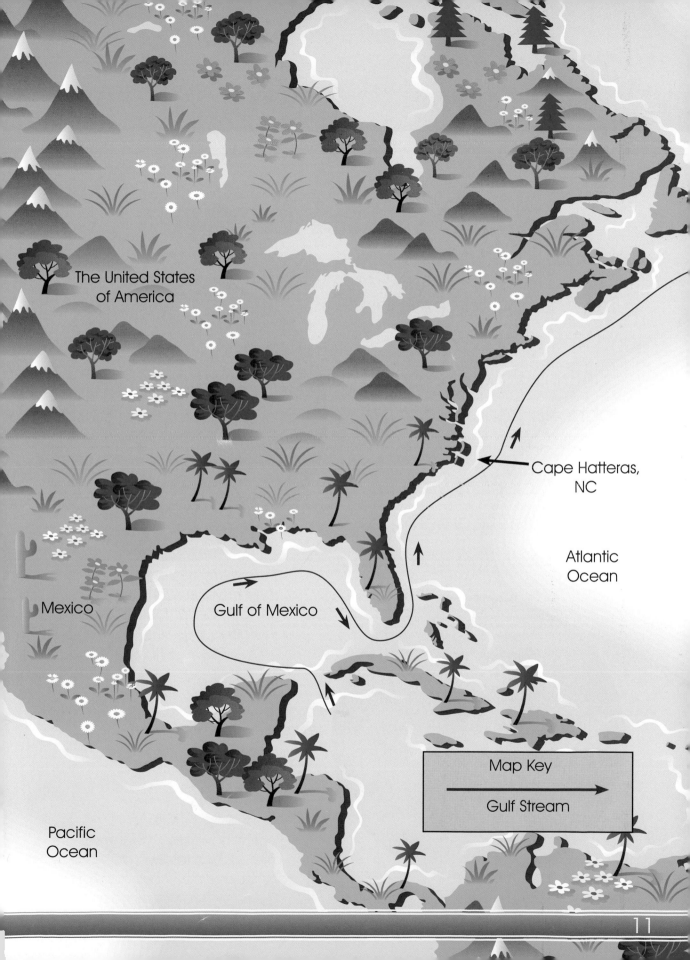

The United States
of America

Mexico

Pacific
Ocean

Gulf of Mexico

Cape Hatteras,
NC

Atlantic
Ocean

Map Key

Gulf Stream

Under the Water

The ocean floor resembles land. The ocean has mountains, valleys, even volcanoes. Trenches form when ocean plates slide and split. Scientists use **submersibles**, cameras, and **sonar** to study the ocean floor.

Teams of scientists build and then travel in submersibles to get a better look at life in the deep blue sea.

National Oceanic and Atmospheric Administration (NOAA) vessels use multi-beam sonar to measure the depth of the seafloor.

Scientists have a lot to learn about the mysterious sea. They are hard at work measuring and mapping the world's ocean trenches. →

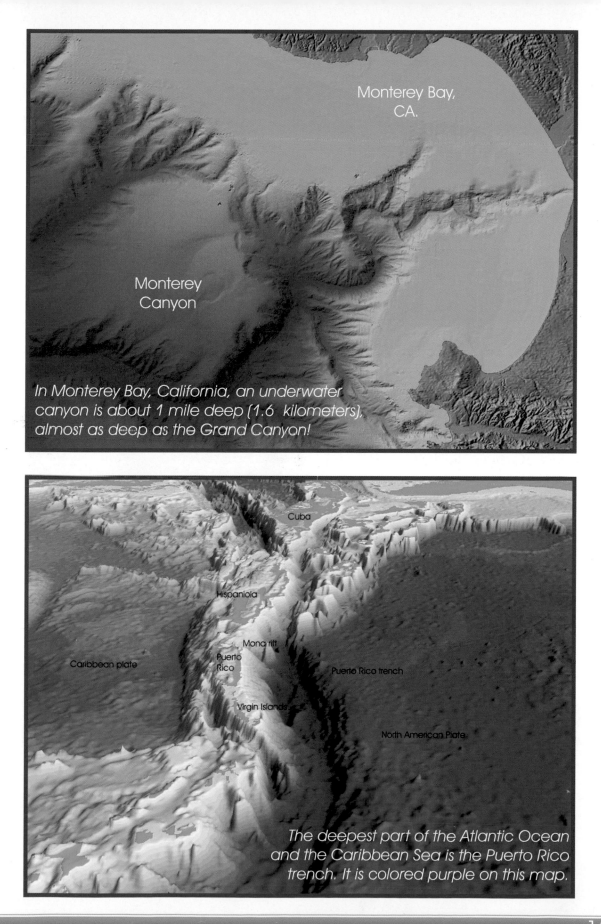

Monterey Bay, CA.

Monterey Canyon

In Monterey Bay, California, an underwater canyon is about 1 mile deep (1.6 kilometers), almost as deep as the Grand Canyon!

Cuba

Hispaniola

Mona rift

Puerto Rico

Caribbean plate

Puerto Rico trench

Virgin Islands

North American Plate

The deepest part of the Atlantic Ocean and the Caribbean Sea is the Puerto Rico trench. It is colored purple on this map.

Animals and Fish

The world's oceans house a variety of wildlife. Turtles, dolphins, whales, eels, and sharks are just a few of the animals under the sea. Some **species**, such as rays, live closer to the surface. Other species, such as the giant squid, live deeper in the ocean where it is much darker.

Stingrays love the warm, shallow waters near beaches.

Found in Hawaii, the Whitemouth Moray Eel makes its home in the coral.

The Hawksbill sea turtle is one of → at-least half a million marine species.

Fun for Us!

Many people enjoy living or vacationing near shorelines because oceans provide lots of fun things to do. People like to boat, fish, surf, scuba dive, snorkel, and swim.

People enjoy the water; however, they often leave trash behind them. Bottles, bags, glass, and plastics **pollute** the ocean and harm marine life.

People use boats to travel far off shore to deep sea fish.

Close to the shore, people hop on surfboards and surf the wild waves.

An exciting way to see ocean life up close is by scuba diving. It takes → practice to learn how to use the equipment needed to scuba dive!

Fishing and Farming

Oceans provide fish and plants for people to eat. Millions of tons of fish come from the ocean to our dinner tables each year. Due to the large demand for fish, the ocean's supply of fish is decreasing.

Fishermen have begun to create fish farms. Fish farmers raise shrimp, clams, oysters, and mussels for people to eat. This protects the species in the ocean. Sometimes disease and bacteria levels are higher in farmed fish. This might be dangerous for humans.

Blue Fin Tuna is one of the most popular fish on menus across the world.

Floating fish farms grow and harvest → fish rather than netting wild fish.

Drill!

Deep under the ocean floor people drill in search of oil. Large offshore oil platforms collect millions of barrels of oil. Tankers transport the oil to refineries. Refineries create **petroleum** and gasoline.

Gas tankers transport oil to refineries.

Offshore oil rigs drill for oil. This can be dangerous work for people and the ocean. In April 2010, a oil rig exploded and leaked oil all over the Gulf of Mexico. →

Protecting Our Oceans

Humans can not live without oceans. However, overfishing, drilling, and pollution cause damage to the intricate **ecosystem**.

You can help protect the world's oceans. Write to your **politicians** and encourage them to fund preservation projects. Pick up your trash so that it does not end up in the ocean. Volunteer in a coastal cleanup. The health of our oceans depends on each and every one of us.

Visit www.usa.gov to find the addresses of your local politicians. Tell them you want them to protect our waterways!

You can help protect our oceans by setting the example. Always throw your trash away!

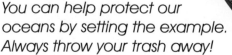

Glossary

ecosystem (EE-koh-siss-tuhm): a community of plants and animals

geographic (jee-OH-graf-ik): earth or land

gravity (GRAV-uh-tee): force that pulls objects toward the Earth

meteorologists (mee-tee-uh-OL-oh-jistz): people who study weather and climate

petroleum (puh-TROH-lee-uhm): thick liquid used to make kerosene, heating oil, and gasoline

politicians (pol-uh-TISH-uhnz): people who hold government offices

pollute (puh-LOOT): to make dirty

sonar (SOH-nar): instrument that sends sound waves through the water to measure depth and chart objects

species (SPEE-sheez): groups of animals that have similar traits

submersibles (sub-MUR-suh-buhlz): ships that can operate under water

Index

Atlantic Ocean   4, 11, 13
Arctic Ocean   4
current(s)   10
farming   18
fishing   18
Gulf Stream   10, 11
Indian Ocean   4

Moon   8
oil   20
Pacific Ocean   4, 11
pollution   22
Southern Ocean   4
tide(s)   8, 9

Websites to Visit

www.kids.nationalgeographic.com/Photos/Gallery/Oceans
www.oceanservice.noaa.gov/education/welcome.html
www.school.discoveryeducation.com/schooladventures/planetocean/

About the Author

Precious McKenzie was born in Ohio, but grew up near the Gulf of Mexico. She loves water sports and walking near the ocean. She tries to help keep our oceans clean by volunteering in coastal cleanups.